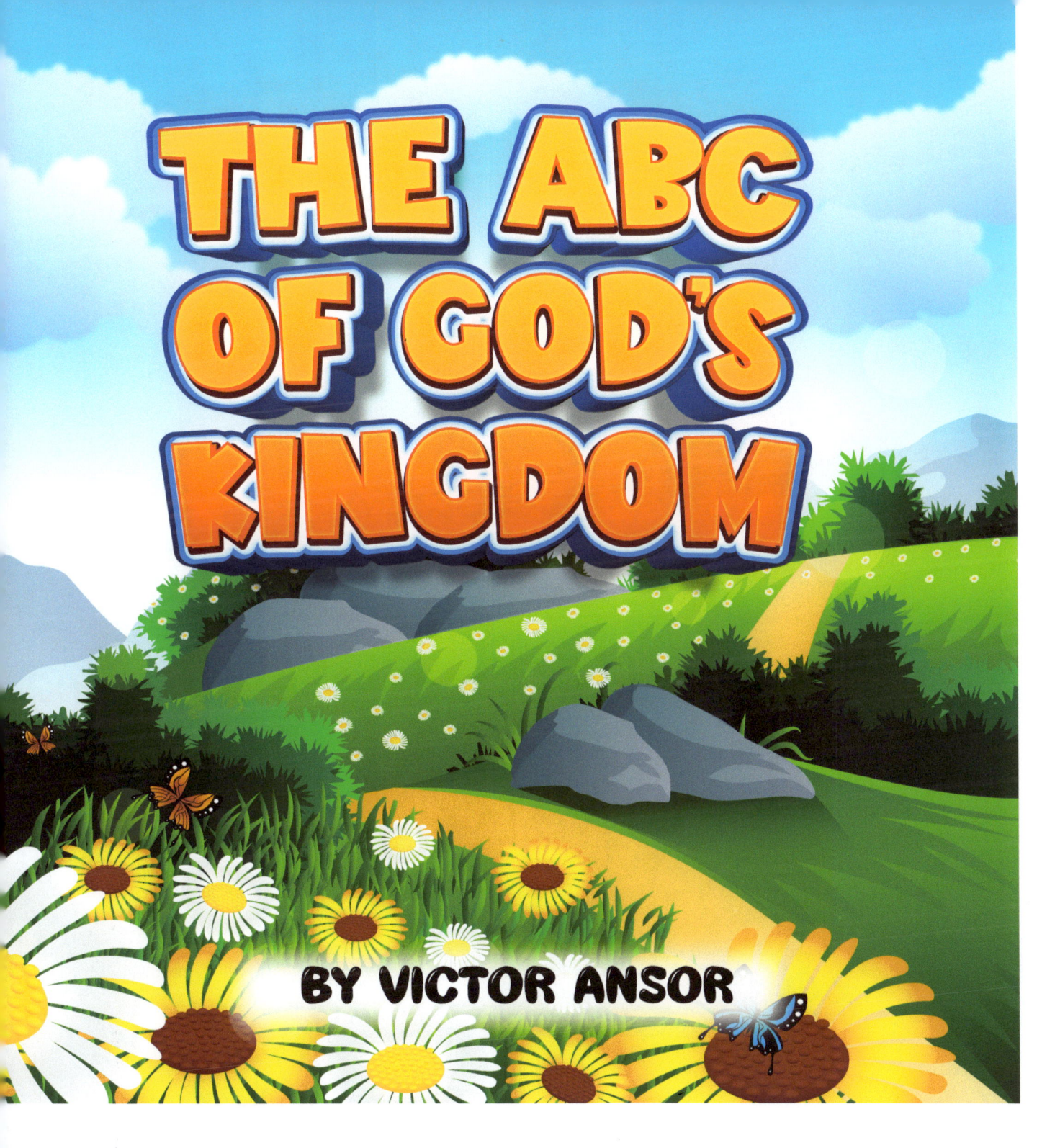

A
ALPHA

I am Alpha and Omega, the beginning and the end, the first and the last.
Revelation 22:13

B
BORN AGAIN

Jesus replied, "Very truly I tell you, no one can see the kingdom of God unless they are born again.
John 3:3

C

CHRISTIAN

The disciples were called Christians first at Antioch.
Acts 11:26

D
DISCIPLE

Then Jesus said to his disciples, "Whoever wants to be my disciple must deny themselves and take up their cross and follow me.
Matthew 16:24

E
EVANGELIZE

He said to them, "Go into all the world and preach the gospel to all creation.
Mark 16:15

F
FAITH

And without faith it is impossible to please God, because anyone who comes to him must believe that he exists and that he rewards those who earnestly seek him.
Hebrews 11:6

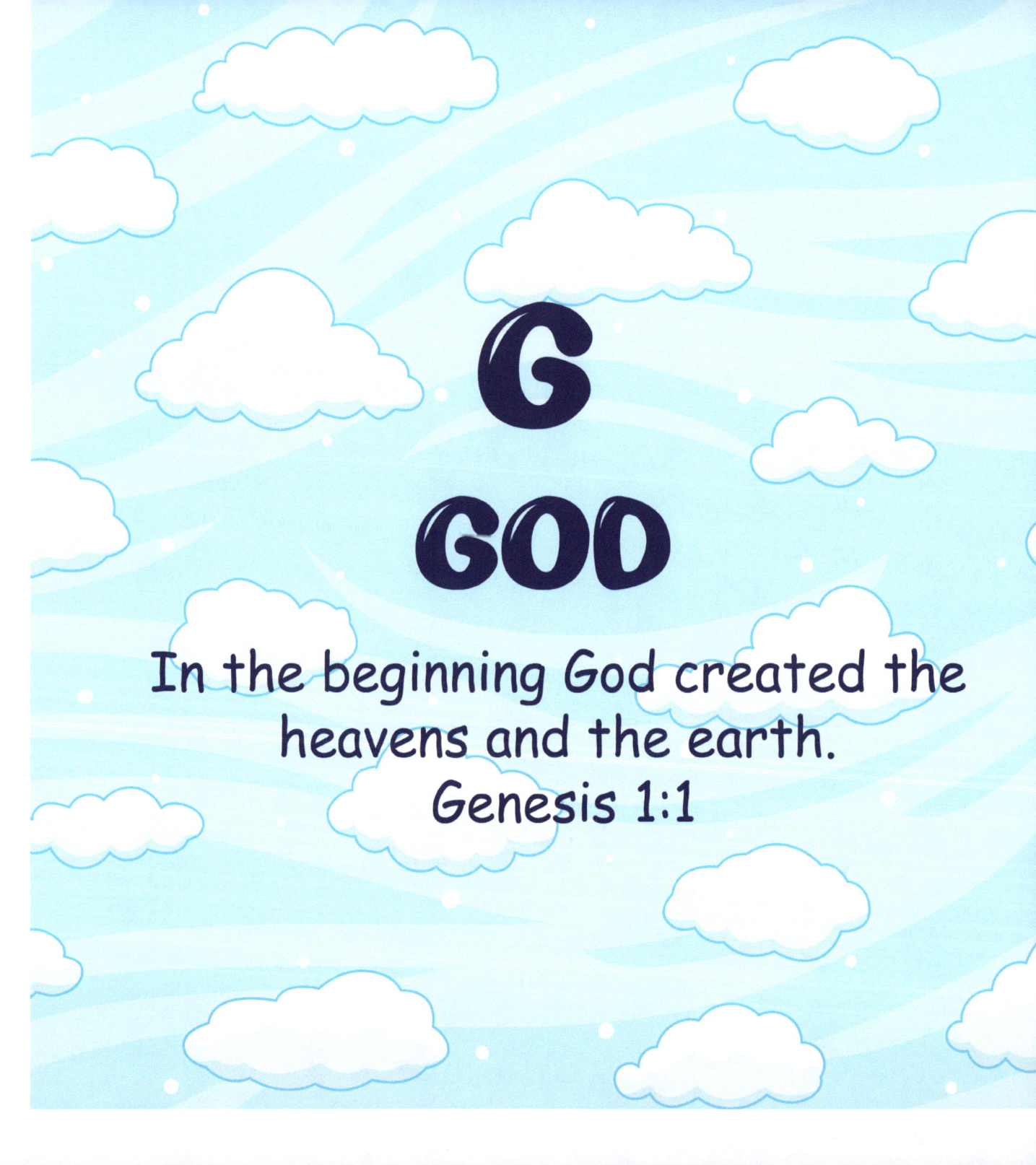

G
GOD

In the beginning God created the heavens and the earth.
Genesis 1:1

H
HOLY SPIRIT

Do you not know that your bodies are temples of the Holy Spirit, who is in you, whom you have received from God? You are not your own.
1 Corinthians 6:19

J
JESUS

She will give birth to a son, and you will call him Jesus, because he will save his people from their sins.
Matthew 1:21

K
KINDNESS

Be kind one to another, tenderhearted, forgiving one another, even as God for Christ's sake has forgiven you.
Ephesians 4:32

M
MONEY

For the love of money is the root of all kinds of evil. Some people, eager for money, have wandered from the faith and pierced themselves with many griefs.
1 Timothy 6:10

N
NEW BIRTH

Therefore, if any man be in Christ, he is a new creature: old things are passed away; behold, all things are become new.
2 Corinthians 5:17

O
OPPORTUNITY

Therefore, as we have opportunity, let us do good to all people, especially to those who belong to the family of believers.
Galatians 6:10

P
POWER

But you will receive power when the Holy Spirit comes on you; and you will be my witnesses in Jerusalem, and in all Judea and Samaria, and to the ends of the earth.
Acts 1:8

Q
QUIET

Make it your ambition to lead a quiet life: You should mind your own business and work with your hands, just as we told you,
1 Thessalonians 4:11

R
RESSURECTION

Jesus said unto her, I am the resurrection, and the life: he that believe in me, though he were dead, yet shall he live.
John 11:25

S

SALVATION

Salvation can be found in no one else. Throughout the whole world, no other name has been given among humans through which we must be saved.
Acts 4:12

T

TRUTH

And you shall know the truth, and the truth shall make you free.
John 8:32

U
UNDERSTANDING

Good understanding wins favor [from others], But the way of the unfaithful is hard [like barren, dry soil].
Proverbs 13:15

V
VICTORY

For everyone born of God overcomes the world. This is the victory that has overcome the world, even our faith.
1 John 5:4

W
WRESTLE

For we wrestle not against flesh and blood, but against principalities, against powers, against the rulers of the darkness of this world, against spiritual wickedness in high places.
Ephesians 6:12

X

CHRIST

Therefore, let all Israel know beyond question that God has made this Jesus, whom you crucified, both Lord and Christ.
Acts 2:36

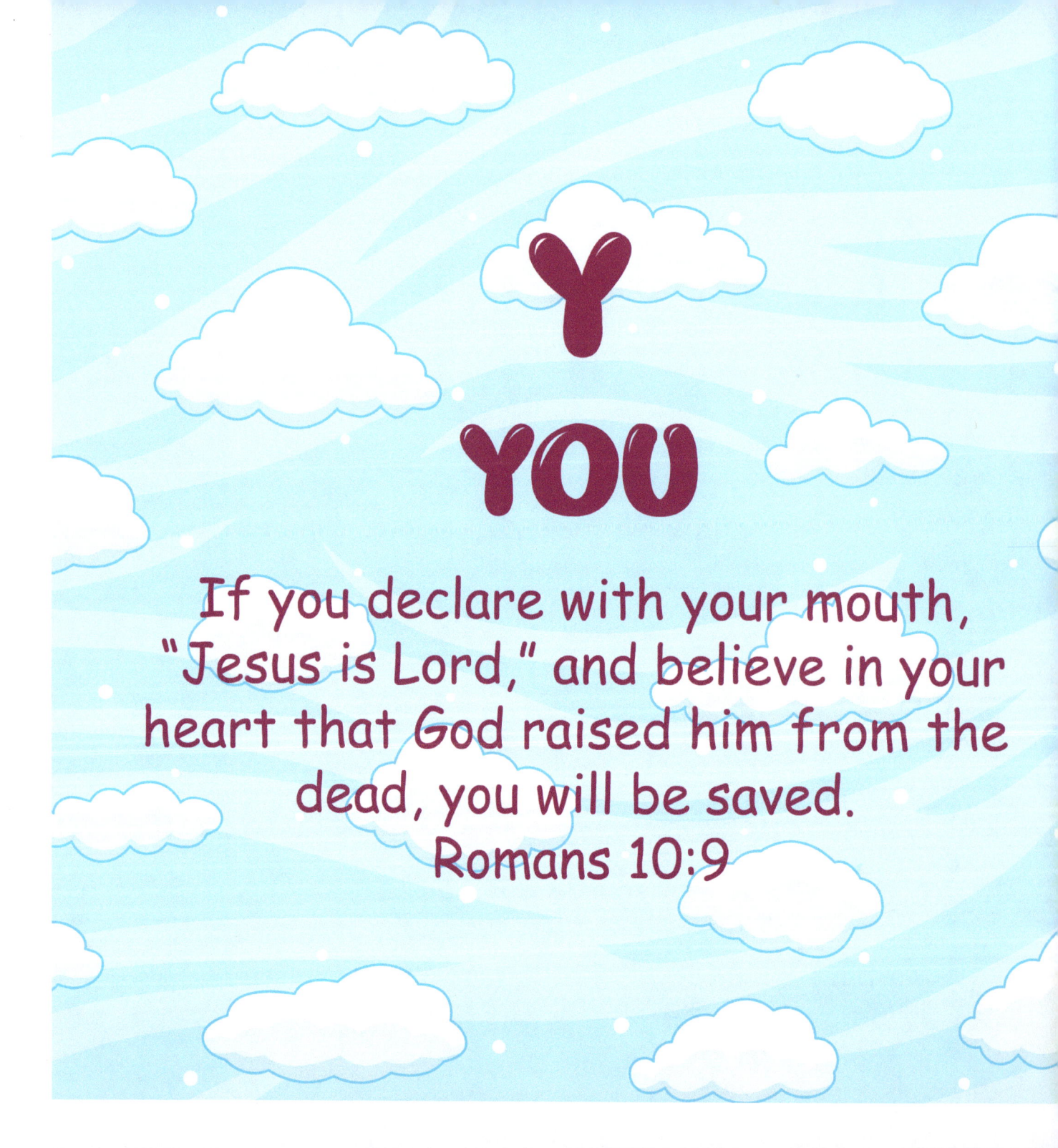

Y

YOU

If you declare with your mouth, "Jesus is Lord," and believe in your heart that God raised him from the dead, you will be saved.
Romans 10:9

Z
ZION

But upon mount Zion shall be deliverance, and there shall be holiness; and the house of Jacob shall possess their possessions.
Obadiah 1:17

www.ingramcontent.com/pod-product-compliance
Lightning Source LLC
Chambersburg PA
CBHW041705160426
43209CB00017B/1756